DECLUTTER & DEFEND

The Essential Guide to Digital Minimalism and Data Privacy for Non-Techies

Alessio rocchI

Table of Contents

Introduction: Welcome to a Calmer, Safer Digital Life

A brief overview of the modern digital dilemma—overwhelming digital clutter and increasing data vulnerabilities. This introduction explains why embracing digital minimalism and safeguarding your personal data are crucial steps toward enhanced productivity, reduced stress, and greater peace of mind.

Chapter 1: The Digital Dilemma

Explore the challenges of our hyper-connected world. This chapter examines the impact of digital overload on mental clarity and productivity while introducing the risks associated with unmanaged data and online exposure.

Chapter 2: Digital Minimalism 101

An accessible introduction to the principles of digital minimalism. Learn what it means to live intentionally in a digital age, discover the benefits of simplifying your online life, and assess your current digital habits.

Chapter 3: Decluttering Your Digital World

A practical, step-by-step guide to purging unnecessary digital baggage. From streamlining your email inbox and organizing digital files to evaluating and reducing app and social media overload, this chapter provides actionable tips and tools for immediate improvement.

Chapter 4: Understanding Data Privacy

Delve into the essentials of data privacy without the technical jargon. This chapter explains key concepts, common threats, and why protecting your personal information is vital in today's digital environment.

Chapter 5: Building Your Digital Defense

Learn the foundational cybersecurity measures that every non-techie can implement. Topics include effective password management, setting up two-factor authentication, and basic data encryption—all explained in plain language with practical examples.

Chapter 6: Managing Your Online Footprint

Discover how to take control of your digital presence. This chapter offers strategies for managing and minimizing your online footprint, including optimizing privacy settings on social media, controlling personal data exposure, and techniques for digital reputation management.

Chapter 7: Essential Tools and Apps for a Minimalist and Secure Digital Life

A curated review of user-friendly apps and software designed to help you maintain a clutter-free digital environment and robust data privacy. Learn which tools best suit your needs and budget, with clear guidance on setup and usage.

Chapter 8: Developing Sustainable Digital Habits

Transition from one-time fixes to long-term digital wellbeing. This chapter provides strategies for establishing routines and practices that keep your digital life organized and secure, including regular digital audits and continual updates on cybersecurity best practices.

Chapter 9: Looking Ahead: The Future of Digital Wellbeing

An exploration of emerging trends in digital minimalism and data privacy. Prepare for upcoming technological changes and learn proactive strategies to keep your digital habits efficient and your data secure in an ever-evolving digital landscape.

Conclusion: Your Path Forward—Embrace a Simplified, Secure Digital Life

A motivational wrap-up that revisits key insights from the book and encourages readers to implement the strategies learned. This conclusion reinforces the benefits of a clutter-free digital space and strong personal data protection, inspiring you to take decisive action toward a healthier digital lifestyle.

Appendices

Introduction

Welcome to a Calmer, Safer Digital Life

The Digital Chaos We Live In

We live in an era of unprecedented digital connectivity. As of 2024, the average person spends over seven hours per day interacting with digital content, and more than 5 billion people worldwide use the internet. With a few taps on a screen, we can communicate across continents, access limitless information, and store entire libraries in a device that fits in the palm of our hands. With a few taps on a screen, we can communicate across continents, access limitless information, and store entire libraries in a device that fits in the palm of our hands. The marvels of the digital age have undoubtedly improved our lives in ways unimaginable just a few decades ago. Yet, for many of us, the same technology designed to liberate us has become a source of stress, distraction, and even vulnerability.

Dozens—sometimes hundreds—of notifications bombard us daily, urging us to check our emails, update our social media, respond to messages, or engage with an endless stream of content. Our smartphones, initially conceived as tools of convenience, have transformed into constant demands on our attention, pulling us in different directions and fragmenting our focus. Meanwhile, lurking beneath the surface of this digital clutter is an even greater concern: the vast amount of personal data we unknowingly share and expose to potential risks.

If you have ever felt overwhelmed by the sheer volume of digital content in your life or worried about your online security but felt powerless to address it, you are not alone. This book will guide you through an essential transformation—one that will empower you to reclaim control over your digital space while ensuring that your personal information remains protected from prying eyes.

The Intersection of Digital Minimalism and Data Privacy

Before diving into the details, it's important to recognize the broader context: Our digital lives are deeply interconnected, and every interaction we have online shapes our overall experience. Many people see digital minimalism and cybersecurity as separate pursuits. Digital minimalists aim to declutter their digital lives, reducing unnecessary distractions to achieve greater focus, productivity, and well-being. Cybersecurity enthusiasts, on the other hand, focus on protecting data, securing accounts, and mitigating digital risks. But what if these two disciplines are actually two sides of the same coin?

By embracing a lifestyle that minimizes digital excess, we automatically reduce the number of touchpoints where our data is vulnerable. For example, maintaining dozens of online accounts increases the likelihood of a data breach—if just one of those accounts is compromised, hackers can use the stolen credentials to gain access to multiple other accounts through password reuse attacks. Reducing unnecessary accounts and subscriptions significantly lowers this risk. Think about it—fewer accounts mean fewer data breaches to worry about. Reducing social media engagement lessens the amount of personal information we expose to third parties. Unsubscribing from dozens of newsletters decreases the chances of phishing scams and email tracking.

This book is designed to help you strike the perfect balance between simplicity and security. Rather than bombarding you with impractical advice or technical jargon, we will focus on actionable, easy-to-implement steps that allow you to enjoy the benefits of digital technology without its burdens.

What You Will Gain from This Book

By the time you finish reading, you will have achieved the following:

- **A clear, structured approach to digital minimalism**: You'll know exactly how to streamline your digital life, declutter your devices, and adopt sustainable minimalist habits.
- **A firm grasp on data privacy and online security**: Without being a cybersecurity expert, you'll understand the most important principles of personal data protection.
- **Practical strategies to reduce digital distractions**: Learn how to use technology intentionally instead of letting it control you.
- **A healthier relationship with your digital devices**: Gain insights into how digital habits affect your mental well-being and productivity.
- **A long-term system for maintaining digital order**: The principles in this book are designed for lasting change, not temporary fixes.

These goals will help you create a balanced, intentional, and secure digital existence, giving you peace of mind and greater control over your technology.

Breaking Free from Digital Overload

It's not just about convenience—your mental well-being is at stake. Studies have shown that excessive digital engagement can lead to increased anxiety, reduced attention spans, and even disrupted sleep patterns. A 2022 study by the American Psychological Association found that individuals who spend more than six hours per day on digital devices report 30% higher levels of stress and anxiety compared to those who limit screen time to two hours or less. When our devices and online presence are filled with digital clutter, it becomes difficult to focus on what truly matters—whether it's work, relationships, or personal growth.

A cluttered digital environment mirrors a cluttered mind. Constantly responding to emails, scrolling through never-ending feeds, and managing a plethora of online accounts takes up cognitive bandwidth, leaving little room for creativity, deep thinking, or genuine relaxation. Digital minimalism is not about rejecting technology; it's about using it with purpose and intentionality.

Understanding the Hidden Dangers of Poor Data Hygiene

While digital clutter is easy to recognize, the dangers of poor data hygiene are often invisible—until it's too late. Have you ever wondered how much personal information is floating around on the internet? Your name, email addresses, purchase history, browsing habits, location data, and even private messages are often stored in places you may not be aware of.

Cybercriminals exploit this data in various ways—identity theft, financial fraud, targeted phishing attacks, and even personal blackmail. While high-profile data breaches make headlines, everyday users suffer the consequences of weak privacy practices all the time. A hacked email account, an exposed password, or a mistakenly shared private photo can have serious repercussions.

Understanding data privacy doesn't mean becoming paranoid—it means becoming informed. With just a few simple adjustments, you can drastically improve your online security without sacrificing the convenience of digital tools.

The Road Ahead

This book is divided into two major parts: **Digital Minimalism** and **Data Privacy & Security**. In the first section, you'll learn how to streamline your digital life, reduce distractions, and cultivate intentional technology habits to improve focus and productivity. The second section will guide you through essential data privacy practices, equipping you with the knowledge to secure your personal information, protect against cyber threats, and navigate the digital world with confidence. You'll begin by learning how to declutter and streamline your digital life, making space for what truly matters. Then, we'll move into practical, non-technical strategies for strengthening your personal cybersecurity and reducing your exposure to digital threats.

The key takeaway? You don't have to choose between convenience and security. By implementing small, intentional changes, you can create a digital life that is both simple and safe.

As you move forward, remember that every step—no matter how small—makes a difference. You don't need to overhaul your entire digital presence overnight. Instead, commit to gradual improvements. The journey to a calmer, safer digital life starts here. Let's begin.

Chapter 1

The Digital Dilemma

Introduction: The Overwhelming Reality of the Digital Age

The modern world is a marvel of digital connectivity, yet it often feels more like a chaotic storm than a well-orchestrated symphony. Our devices, designed to enhance our lives, have become sources of distraction, stress, and even anxiety. A 2023 study by Asurion found that the average person checks their phone 352 times per day—an increase of over 4x from a decade ago. This constant digital engagement has been linked to increased anxiety levels, reduced productivity, and a heightened sense of dependency on technology. The average person checks their phone over 96 times a day, and studies show that prolonged screen time is linked to decreased attention spans, disrupted sleep patterns, and heightened levels of stress.

We didn't arrive at this state overnight. Over the past two decades, rapid technological advancements have profoundly altered the way we communicate, work, and manage our personal lives. However, while technology has improved efficiency and convenience, it has also burdened us with an overabundance of information, relentless notifications, and increasing digital vulnerabilities.

This chapter will explore the growing problem of digital overload, how it affects our mental well-being, productivity, and personal security, and why taking control of our digital habits is essential to living a more intentional, balanced life.

The Rise of Digital Overload

The Evolution of Our Digital Lives

The early 2000s introduced a wave of technological breakthroughs that revolutionized how we interact with the world. The rise of social media, smartphones, and cloud computing reshaped our lives, blurring the lines between work and personal time. What was once a tool for occasional convenience has transformed into an omnipresent force that demands our constant attention.

Consider the way we consume information today compared to just a decade ago. In 2011, the average person encountered about five times more daily information than in 1986. The explosion of digital content—emails, news feeds, social media updates, streaming platforms—has created an environment of perpetual input, leaving us feeling mentally exhausted before the day even begins.

Why More Information Doesn't Mean More Knowledge

Paradoxically, despite having access to endless information at our fingertips, we are less informed than ever. This occurs due to cognitive overload, where our brains struggle to filter essential information amidst the constant influx of content. Additionally, the rise of misinformation and algorithm-driven content curation often prioritizes engagement over accuracy, making it harder to discern credible sources. The constant influx of content has led to "information fatigue," where our brains struggle to filter what is relevant and meaningful. Studies indicate that excessive exposure to digital media reduces our ability to retain information and make critical decisions effectively. In essence, our minds are so preoccupied with processing data that deep thinking and reflection have become rare commodities.

The Psychological Toll of Digital Overstimulation

How Constant Connectivity Fuels Anxiety

Notifications, emails, and social media alerts act as digital breadcrumbs, constantly pulling our focus in different directions. This state of hyper-connectivity triggers the brain's stress response, leading to heightened levels of cortisol—the stress hormone. Over time, this can contribute to chronic stress, fatigue, and even burnout.

Consider the case of "phantom vibration syndrome," where individuals perceive phone vibrations even when no notification exists. A 2017 study published in the Journal of Computers in Human Behavior found that nearly 90% of participants had experienced phantom vibrations, highlighting how our brains adapt to constant digital stimulation. Personally, I recall a friend who, after a week-long vacation without her phone, still felt her leg "buzzing"—a testament to how deeply ingrained these habits become. This phenomenon highlights how deeply ingrained digital habits have become, rewiring our brains to expect constant stimulation. The inability to disconnect leads to a feeling of restlessness, making it difficult to focus on deep work or relax fully.

The Impact on Sleep and Cognitive Function

Blue light emitted from screens interferes with melatonin production, disrupting our natural sleep cycles. A study from Harvard Medical School found that individuals who use screens late at night experience lower-quality sleep, reduced REM cycles, and increased grogginess the next day. Poor sleep has a cascading effect on cognitive function, impairing memory retention, problem-solving skills, and emotional regulation.

Digital overstimulation also affects our attention spans. In 2000, the average human attention span was 12 seconds; by 2021, it had dropped to just 8.25 seconds—shorter than that of a goldfish. The more we condition our brains to operate in rapid, short bursts of information, the harder it becomes to engage in prolonged focus, critical thinking, or creative problem-solving.

Digital Clutter and Its Hidden Costs

The Problem with Endless Digital Hoarding

Our digital environments are often as cluttered as our physical spaces. Think of an overflowing email inbox with thousands of unread messages, a desktop filled with disorganized files, or a phone cluttered with apps you never use. These digital messes create cognitive overload, making it harder to focus, find important information, and maintain mental clarity. The sheer volume of unused apps, duplicate files, and endless email subscriptions clogs our devices and clouds our mental clarity. Studies have shown that digital clutter contributes to cognitive overload, leading to decision fatigue and decreased productivity.

Beyond that, excess digital clutter poses security risks. Old accounts, forgotten subscriptions, and unused platforms serve as entry points for cybercriminals. Data breaches often occur due to forgotten, weak, or reused passwords linked to dormant accounts. Without regular digital maintenance, our personal information becomes more vulnerable than we realize.

How a Cluttered Digital Life Drains Productivity

Switching between tasks, also known as "context switching," is one of the biggest productivity killers. Each time we shift our focus from one digital task to another—checking emails, responding to messages, browsing social media—it takes an average of 23 minutes to regain full concentration. The cumulative effect is staggering, significantly reducing our efficiency and effectiveness throughout the day.

A study conducted by the University of California, Irvine, found that workers who frequently switched between tasks reported higher levels of stress and mental exhaustion. In contrast, those who minimized digital interruptions performed better in deep work, maintaining greater focus and efficiency.

The Hidden Dangers of Digital Dependency

The Illusion of Productivity

In today's work culture, being constantly online is often mistaken for being productive. But responding to emails at all hours, checking notifications immediately, and multitasking between numerous applications create the illusion of busyness rather than actual productivity.

A key example is the rise of "email debt," where individuals feel pressured to respond instantly to messages, leaving them with little time for focused, meaningful work. Studies show that professionals spend an average of 28% of their workweek managing emails—a massive drain on productivity.

The Privacy and Security Trade-Off

Beyond productivity concerns, our increasing dependence on digital platforms raises serious privacy and security risks. Every app we download, every social media post we make, and every online service we sign up for contributes to our "digital footprint." This data is often collected, sold, and used by corporations, governments, and cybercriminals for various purposes.

Public Wi-Fi networks, unsecured cloud storage, and lax password habits expose personal and financial information to potential cyber threats. With identity theft and data breaches on the rise, understanding how to minimize unnecessary digital exposure is crucial for long-term security.

Taking Back Control: Steps Toward a Healthier Digital Life

Building Awareness and Setting Intentions

The first step toward digital minimalism and security is awareness. Conducting a digital audit—assessing how and where you spend your digital time—helps identify areas that need improvement. By setting clear intentions for how technology serves you, rather than the other way around, you can begin making intentional choices that enhance your life.

Practical Steps to Reduce Digital Overload

- **Batch Process Notifications:** Instead of responding to notifications in real-time, allocate specific times during the day to check messages and emails.

- **Declutter Your Digital Space:** Regularly delete unused apps, organize files, and unsubscribe from unnecessary email lists.
- **Schedule Screen-Free Time:** Set boundaries for technology use, such as implementing a "no-phone zone" during meals or before bedtime.
- **Strengthen Security Habits:** Use unique passwords for different accounts, enable two-factor authentication, and be mindful of the data you share online.

Conclusion: The Path Forward

Our digital dilemma is not an inevitable consequence of technology—it is the result of unconscious habits and unchecked digital consumption. By becoming intentional with how we engage with technology, we can regain control, improve focus, and protect our personal information. This means taking active steps to manage our screen time, reducing unnecessary digital clutter, and being mindful of the information we share online. Establishing clear boundaries with technology, setting digital detox periods, and strengthening cybersecurity habits are all critical components of this journey. By implementing these strategies, we can cultivate a healthier relationship with technology and reclaim our mental clarity and security in an increasingly digital world. The journey toward a calmer, safer digital life starts with small, deliberate steps.

The next chapter will guide you through the fundamentals of digital minimalism, providing actionable strategies to streamline your digital existence and reclaim your mental clarity. Let's take the first step toward a balanced digital future.

Chapter 2

Digital Minimalism 101

Introduction: The Power of Intentional Technology Use

In an era where digital devices dictate much of our daily lives, few people stop to consider how their technology use aligns with their personal values and priorities. Digital minimalism is more than just decluttering apps or reducing screen time—it's a philosophy of intentional technology use that fosters focus, creativity, and well-being.

This chapter will introduce the core principles of digital minimalism, explore its benefits, and provide a practical roadmap for implementing a more intentional and fulfilling digital lifestyle. By the end of this chapter, you will understand how to regain control over your digital world, allowing technology to serve you rather than the other way around.

Understanding Digital Minimalism

What is Digital Minimalism?

Digital minimalism is a deliberate approach to using technology that prioritizes meaningful engagement while eliminating unnecessary digital distractions. For example, consider a freelance writer who struggled with constant notifications and a cluttered inbox, leading to decreased productivity and creative burnout. After implementing digital minimalism, they reduced their online accounts, disabled unnecessary alerts, and scheduled dedicated focus hours—ultimately regaining control over their workflow and mental clarity. Unlike digital detoxes, which offer temporary relief from digital overload, digital minimalism is a long-term lifestyle choice that fosters mindfulness and intentionality in how we engage with digital tools.

The goal is not to eliminate technology but to optimize its use so that it enhances rather than detracts from our lives. A digital minimalist carefully curates their digital environment, ensuring that every app, platform, and device serves a clear and valuable purpose.

The Three Core Principles of Digital Minimalism

1. **Intentional Use** – Every piece of technology should have a clear purpose that aligns with personal or professional goals.
2. **Quality Over Quantity** – Prioritize deep, meaningful digital interactions over mindless scrolling and information overload.

3. **Control Over Consumption** – Instead of letting digital platforms dictate behavior, take charge of how and when technology is used.

The Benefits of Digital Minimalism

Increased Focus and Productivity

The modern digital landscape thrives on distraction. From social media notifications to endless email threads, constant digital interruptions fragment our attention and reduce our ability to engage in deep work. Research has shown that multitasking and frequent task-switching impair cognitive performance, leading to lower efficiency and creativity.

By adopting digital minimalism, you can cultivate an environment that supports sustained focus and higher-quality work. Imagine an open-plan office where employees constantly receive notifications, check emails, and switch between tasks. This fragmented workflow diminishes deep concentration and increases stress. However, by implementing digital minimalism—such as batching emails, setting dedicated focus hours, and disabling unnecessary alerts—workers can reclaim their productivity and reduce mental fatigue. Techniques such as batching digital communications and setting strict notification boundaries can significantly enhance productivity.

Improved Mental Well-Being

Excessive screen time and digital engagement have been linked to higher levels of anxiety, depression, and stress. The constant pressure to stay connected, compare oneself to others on social media, and process vast amounts of digital information takes a toll on mental health.

Digital minimalism fosters a more balanced relationship with technology, allowing space for offline experiences, deeper relationships, and mental clarity. Practicing mindfulness in technology use leads to improved emotional well-being and reduced digital burnout.

Enhanced Relationships and Social Connections

Meaningful interactions often suffer when digital distractions take precedence over face-to-face communication. Digital minimalism encourages being present in the moment, fostering stronger personal and professional relationships.

Simple changes, such as implementing phone-free meals, designating screen-free times, and prioritizing in-person conversations over digital exchanges, can significantly enhance the quality of relationships.

Practical Steps to Implement Digital Minimalism

Step 1: Conduct a Digital Audit

Before making changes, it's essential to assess the current state of your digital life. A digital audit involves:

- Listing all digital tools, apps, and platforms used daily.
- Identifying which are essential and which contribute to digital clutter.
- Evaluating time spent on various digital activities.
- Recognizing digital habits that lead to stress, distraction, or inefficiency.

Step 2: Declutter Your Digital Space

Once the audit is complete, it's time to declutter. The goal is to remove distractions and streamline technology use.

- **Uninstall Unnecessary Apps** – Remove apps that serve no real purpose or contribute to mindless consumption.

- **Organize Digital Files** – Create structured folders for documents, photos, and emails.
- **Unsubscribe from Unwanted Emails** – Reduce inbox clutter by opting out of newsletters and marketing emails that provide no value.
- **Limit Social Media Accounts** – Keep only the platforms that add meaningful value to your life.

Step 3: Set Boundaries for Digital Use

Technology is most effective when it is used intentionally. Setting boundaries helps regain control over digital interactions.

- **Create Screen-Free Zones** – Designate areas in your home or workplace where digital devices are not allowed.
- **Schedule Tech-Free Time Blocks** – Allocate specific hours for deep work, relaxation, or social activities without digital interruptions.
- **Turn Off Non-Essential Notifications** – Disable alerts that disrupt focus and encourage compulsive checking.
- **Use Digital Tools with Purpose** – Rather than defaulting to social media during downtime, engage in purposeful activities such as reading, exercise, or hobbies.

Step 4: Optimize Digital Consumption

Digital minimalism is not about rejecting technology but curating content that aligns with personal and professional goals.

- **Curate High-Quality Content** – Follow only accounts, blogs, and media sources that provide meaningful insights and inspiration.
- **Adopt a "One-In, One-Out" Rule** – When adding a new app or subscription, remove an existing one to maintain balance.
- **Batch Process Information Intake** – Set specific times to check news, emails, and updates instead of consuming information continuously.
- **Practice Mindful Consumption** – Before engaging in any digital activity, ask: "Is this adding value to my life?"

Sustaining Digital Minimalism as a Lifestyle

Digital minimalism is not a one-time fix but a continuous process of refinement. Sustainable habits ensure long-term success.

Regular Digital Detox Sessions

Periodic breaks from technology help reset digital habits and reinforce intentional use. Consider implementing:

- **Daily Mini-Detoxes** – One-hour screen-free breaks each day. For instance, Sarah, a project manager, found that setting aside an hour each morning before work to read or go for a walk instead of checking emails significantly improved her focus and reduced stress throughout the day.
- **Weekly Digital Sabbaths** – A full day each week without unnecessary technology use.
- **Annual Digital Retreats** – Extended periods of complete disconnection to refresh mental clarity.

Adapting to Life Changes

As career and personal circumstances evolve, so do digital needs. Reevaluate digital habits periodically and adjust strategies accordingly.

Building a Supportive Environment

Surrounding yourself with like-minded individuals who value digital minimalism can reinforce positive behaviors. Consider joining online communities such as the Digital Minimalism subreddit, Facebook groups focused on mindful technology use, or following thought leaders in the space. Engaging in discussions and sharing experiences with others can provide motivation and new strategies to maintain a minimalist digital lifestyle. Encourage family, friends, or coworkers to join in the practice, creating a collective commitment to healthier technology use.

Conclusion: Embracing a More Intentional Digital Life

Digital minimalism offers a pathway to reclaiming control over technology and living with greater purpose. By intentionally curating digital interactions, setting clear boundaries, and fostering mindful consumption, you can create a lifestyle that prioritizes focus, well-being, and meaningful experiences.

The next chapter will delve deeper into digital decluttering strategies, providing step-by-step guidance on simplifying and streamlining your digital environment for maximum efficiency and clarity. For example, one of the simplest but most effective decluttering methods is the "Inbox Zero" approach—managing emails so that your inbox is always empty or near empty, reducing mental load and improving productivity. Get ready to explore more techniques that will help you take back control of your digital space. Let's take the next step toward a more intentional digital future.

Chapter 3

Decluttering Your Digital World

Introduction: The Power of a Simplified Digital Space

In an era where digital clutter competes for our attention at every turn, finding clarity in our digital world is more essential than ever. From overstuffed inboxes and redundant files to a constant flood of notifications, digital excess not only overwhelms but also diminishes our productivity and focus. Just as physical clutter can create stress and inefficiency, digital clutter silently erodes our mental clarity, leaving us feeling disorganized and drained. Imagine a desk covered in stacks of paper, post-it notes, and tangled cords—it's difficult to find what you need and focus on work. Similarly, an overloaded inbox, dozens of browser tabs, and a phone filled with unused apps create digital chaos that can be just as distracting and overwhelming.

This chapter will take you through a structured, step-by-step approach to decluttering every aspect of your digital life. Whether you want to optimize your inbox, streamline your file organization, or regain control over your online presence, this guide will equip you with the practical strategies necessary to transform your digital space into an oasis of order and efficiency.

The Hidden Costs of Digital Clutter

The Psychological and Productivity Toll

We often underestimate the impact of digital clutter on our mental well-being. When our devices are filled with excessive notifications, a barrage of emails, or disorganized files, our cognitive load increases. Studies have shown that information overload leads to higher stress levels and impairs our ability to concentrate on meaningful work. A study conducted by the University of California, Irvine, found that workers who are frequently interrupted by digital distractions take an average of 23 minutes to refocus on their original task, contributing to decreased productivity and increased mental fatigue. The more fragmented our attention, the less effective we become at completing important tasks.

Security Risks of Digital Overload

Beyond mental fatigue, digital clutter can be a security risk. Old accounts, forgotten subscriptions, and unmonitored applications can serve as backdoors for cyber threats. Hackers often exploit weak security measures in unused accounts, potentially compromising personal or financial data. Regularly auditing and decluttering your digital environment is not just about efficiency—it's about safeguarding your privacy.

Step 1: Organizing Your Digital Files and Folders

The Digital Filing System Method

Start by structuring your digital files just as you would organize a physical filing cabinet. Implement a simple yet effective hierarchy:

1. **Main Categories:** Create high-level folders such as Work, Personal, Finance, and Projects.
2. **Subfolders for Specificity:** Inside each main folder, create subfolders for better classification. For example, under "Work," you might have "Reports," "Presentations," and "Client Documents."
3. **Consistent Naming Conventions:** Use clear and consistent file names, such as "2024_Tax_Return.pdf" instead of "Doc1.pdf."
4. **Eliminate Redundant Files:** Delete duplicates and outdated files regularly to keep your system lean and navigable.

Automating File Management

To maintain long-term order, leverage automation tools like:

- **Google Drive or OneDrive Backup** – Automatically sync important files to cloud storage.
- **Hazel (Mac) or File Juggler (Windows)** – Automate file organization based on pre-set rules.
- **Duplicate File Finders** – Use software like CCleaner or Gemini to remove redundant files and free up storage space.

Step 2: Streamlining Your Email Inbox

The Inbox Zero Approach

A cluttered inbox is one of the biggest sources of digital stress. The Inbox Zero method helps regain control over emails and minimize digital fatigue. Imagine starting your day with hundreds of unread emails, feeling overwhelmed before even beginning your tasks. After implementing Inbox Zero, you wake up to a streamlined inbox, where only important messages remain, and everything else is neatly archived or categorized. This shift not only reduces stress but also enhances productivity by allowing you to focus on meaningful work rather than constantly managing emails.

1. **Unsubscribe Ruthlessly:** Use tools like Unroll.Me or Clean Email to unsubscribe from unnecessary newsletters and promotional emails.
2. **Create Smart Filters and Labels:** Automate sorting by setting up filters for priority emails, receipts, and personal correspondence.
3. **Use the Two-Minute Rule:** If an email can be responded to in under two minutes, address it immediately.
4. **Set Designated Email Times:** Instead of reacting to emails constantly, allocate specific time blocks for checking and responding to messages.
5. **Archive Instead of Hoard:** If an email doesn't require immediate action, archive it for future reference rather than keeping it in your inbox.

Step 3: Decluttering Your Digital Devices

App Audit and Optimization

Most of us download apps we rarely use, leading to an overwhelming number of icons cluttering our screens and consuming storage. Setting a monthly reminder to review and delete unused apps can help keep devices organized and efficient, reducing unnecessary digital clutter.

1. **Delete Unused Apps:** Review your phone and computer applications, removing those you haven't used in the last three months.
2. **Rearrange for Efficiency:** Place frequently used apps on the home screen and group similar ones into folders.
3. **Manage Background Apps:** Many apps run in the background, draining battery life and data. Regularly check and disable unnecessary background processes.
4. **Limit Notifications:** Disable notifications for non-essential apps to minimize distractions and interruptions.

Step 4: Managing Your Online Presence

Social Media Cleanup

Our digital identities are often scattered across multiple platforms, many of which we no longer engage with. Conducting a social media audit helps maintain a curated and intentional online presence.

1. **Deactivate Old Accounts:** Use tools like JustDeleteMe to find and close inactive or unnecessary accounts.

2. **Update Privacy Settings:** Regularly review and adjust privacy settings on social media to control who can see your information.

3. **Curate Your Feed:** Unfollow accounts that no longer add value to your life, and prioritize meaningful connections over mindless scrolling.

4. **Use Time Management Tools:** Apps like Freedom or StayFocusd can help set limits on social media usage and reduce digital distractions.

Password and Security Management

A decluttered digital world is a secure digital world. Strengthen your security posture by:

- **Using a Password Manager:** Apps like LastPass or Bitwarden store and generate secure passwords.

- **Enabling Two-Factor Authentication (2FA):** Adds an extra layer of security to prevent unauthorized access.

- **Regularly Reviewing Permissions:** Check which apps have access to your data and remove those that no longer need it.

Step 5: Implementing a Sustainable Digital Decluttering Routine

Decluttering your digital world is not a one-time task—it requires ongoing maintenance. For example, James, a freelance designer, made digital decluttering a weekly ritual. Every Friday, he would review his inbox, delete unnecessary files, and reassess the apps on his phone. Over time, this habit helped him stay organized, improve his workflow, and significantly reduce stress associated with digital clutter. Establish a routine that ensures long-term digital clarity.

Daily Habits for Digital Simplicity

- **5-Minute Inbox Review:** Quickly sort, archive, or delete unnecessary emails at the end of each day.
- **End-of-Day Desktop Cleanup:** Keep your desktop clear of temporary files by storing important documents in designated folders.
- **Limit Nighttime Screen Time:** Reduce blue light exposure by setting screen-free periods before bed.

Weekly and Monthly Digital Checkups

- **Device Storage Cleanup:** Delete temporary files, cache, and unnecessary downloads.

- **Reevaluate Digital Subscriptions:** Cancel unused streaming services or software subscriptions.
- **Reinforce Security Measures:** Update passwords, review security settings, and check for software updates.

Annual Digital Reset

- **Deep Clean Your Cloud Storage:** Organize Google Drive, Dropbox, or iCloud files.
- **Reassess Social Media Presence:** Reflect on which platforms serve you best and make necessary adjustments.
- **Tech Detox Challenge:** Try a 24-hour digital detox to reset your habits and reinforce mindful technology use.

Conclusion: The Freedom of a Clutter-Free Digital Life

Decluttering your digital world is one of the most effective ways to regain mental clarity, boost productivity, and enhance security. By systematically organizing files, streamlining email use, optimizing devices, and managing online presence, you create an environment that fosters focus and efficiency.

As you move forward, remember that digital minimalism is not about deprivation—it's about reclaiming control. With consistent habits and intentional digital engagement, you can build a sustainable, distraction-free digital life that aligns with your goals and values.

In the next chapter, we will explore strategies to set digital boundaries and establish a healthier relationship with technology, ensuring that your digital world remains an asset rather than a source of stress. Let's continue this journey toward a more intentional and empowered digital experience.

Chapter 4

Understanding Data Privacy

Introduction: Why Data Privacy Matters More Than Ever

In the modern digital landscape, data is the new currency. Every click, every purchase, and every online interaction contributes to an ever-growing profile that companies, advertisers, and even cybercriminals can access. As technology evolves, so do the threats and vulnerabilities that compromise our personal and professional data. For example, the 2023 MOVEit data breach exposed sensitive information from multiple government agencies and corporations, highlighting the ongoing risks posed by cyberattacks. Yet, despite the increasing risks, many people remain unaware of how much of their information is exposed or how it is being used.

This chapter will take a deep dive into the principles of data privacy, uncovering how personal data is collected, stored, and shared. We will explore the risks of data breaches, strategies for protecting sensitive information, and the best practices for maintaining control over your digital footprint. By the end of this chapter, you will have a clear understanding of how to safeguard your privacy in a world where data is constantly being mined.

The Fundamentals of Data Privacy

What Is Data Privacy?

Data privacy refers to the protection of personal information from unauthorized access, collection, or use. It encompasses the rights individuals have over their data and the measures they can take to control how it is shared and stored. At its core, data privacy is about maintaining autonomy over personal information and ensuring that sensitive data does not fall into the wrong hands.

Types of Personal Data

Personal data can be categorized into several key areas:

- **Personally Identifiable Information (PII):** This includes your name, address, phone number, and email.
- **Financial Data:** Credit card details, banking information, and payment records.
- **Health Information:** Medical history, prescriptions, and health records.
- **Behavioral Data:** Browsing history, search activity, and purchase behavior.
- **Biometric Data:** Fingerprints, facial recognition, and voice patterns.

Each type of data holds value for different entities—from marketers to hackers—which is why understanding and protecting it is crucial. For example, companies use browsing history and purchase behavior to tailor targeted ads, often leading to eerily specific product recommendations. Meanwhile, cybercriminals exploit stolen financial data for fraudulent transactions or identity theft, causing significant financial and emotional distress for victims.

How Your Data Is Collected and Used

The Digital Footprint You Leave Behind

Every time you use a website, social media platform, or app, you leave behind traces of your digital identity. This collection of data, often referred to as a "digital footprint," is used by businesses, governments, and malicious actors for various purposes.

Common ways your data is collected include:

- **Cookies and Tracking Technologies:** Websites use cookies to track browsing behavior and personalize advertisements.

- **Social Media Platforms:** Every post, like, and comment contributes to a profile of your interests and habits.

- **E-commerce Transactions:** Online purchases generate data that companies use to target you with ads and recommendations.

- **Mobile Apps:** Many apps request unnecessary permissions to access your location, contacts, and device storage.

- **Public Databases:** Government records, voting databases, and property records are often publicly accessible.

How Companies Monetize Your Data

Your personal data is a valuable commodity in the digital marketplace. Companies make billions of dollars by selling consumer data to advertisers, data brokers, and even other corporations. Some of the ways companies monetize your data include:

- **Targeted Advertising:** Social media and search engines analyze your behavior to deliver personalized ads.

- **Data Sharing with Third Parties:** Many services share user data with partner companies for marketing and research.

- **AI and Machine Learning Algorithms:** Companies use your data to improve predictive algorithms that drive recommendations and content personalization.

Illustration Idea: A simple flowchart showing how data moves from users to companies, passing through platforms like social media, e-commerce, and advertising networks.

The Risks of Data Exposure

Cyber Threats and Data Breaches

One of the greatest risks to personal data privacy is cybercrime. A striking example is the 2017 Equifax data breach, which exposed the personal information of nearly 147 million individuals, including Social Security numbers, birthdates, and addresses. This breach not only resulted in massive financial losses but also led to widespread identity theft, demonstrating how a single cybersecurity lapse can have catastrophic consequences for both individuals and businesses. Hackers exploit weak security measures to steal sensitive information, which can lead to identity theft, financial fraud, and personal blackmail.

Notable cyber threats include:

- **Phishing Attacks:** Fraudulent emails and messages designed to trick users into revealing passwords and personal information.
- **Data Breaches:** Large-scale hacks that expose user data from companies, hospitals, and financial institutions.
- **Ransomware Attacks:** Malicious software that encrypts user data, demanding payment to restore access.
- **Man-in-the-Middle Attacks:** Cybercriminals intercept communications between two parties to steal information.

The Dangers of Oversharing Online

Many people unknowingly expose themselves to privacy risks by oversharing on social media and public forums. Personal details such as birthdays, vacation plans, and even location check-ins can be exploited by criminals.

To minimize exposure:

- **Limit the amount of personal information shared online.**
- **Use private settings on social media accounts.**

- Be cautious of sharing photos with identifiable landmarks or addresses.
- Think before posting sensitive or controversial content.

Strategies for Protecting Your Data

Strengthening Account Security

- **Use Strong, Unique Passwords:** Avoid using common passwords and consider using a password manager.
- **Enable Two-Factor Authentication (2FA):** Adds an extra layer of security to prevent unauthorized logins.
- **Regularly Update Software and Apps:** Security vulnerabilities are often patched in updates, so keeping your software up to date is essential.

Enhancing Online Privacy

- **Use a VPN (Virtual Private Network):** Encrypts your internet connection to protect browsing activity from prying eyes.
- **Opt Out of Data Collection:** Many websites and apps allow users to limit data sharing—review privacy settings and adjust accordingly.

- **Be Cautious with Public Wi-Fi:** Avoid accessing sensitive accounts when connected to public networks.

- **Use Privacy-Focused Browsers and Search Engines:** Consider switching to browsers like Brave or DuckDuckGo for enhanced privacy protection.

Conclusion: Taking Control of Your Digital Privacy

Data privacy is no longer optional—it is a necessity in today's digital world. With corporations, hackers, and even governments collecting vast amounts of information, protecting personal data is essential to maintaining security and autonomy.

By understanding how data is collected, recognizing the risks, and implementing proactive security measures, you can significantly reduce your digital exposure and take control of your privacy. The next chapter will explore the most effective tools and apps for maintaining digital security, helping you build a fortified defense against cyber threats and data exploitation.

Taking charge of your digital privacy today means securing a safer, more private tomorrow.

Chapter 5

Building Your Digital Defense

Introduction: Why Digital Security is No Longer Optional

The modern digital world is a battlefield. In 2023 alone, cybercrime caused over $8 trillion in damages worldwide, making it one of the most pressing security challenges of our time. From phishing scams targeting everyday users to sophisticated ransomware attacks crippling businesses, digital threats continue to evolve and escalate. With cybercriminals constantly devising new tactics to exploit personal data, digital security is no longer a luxury—it is a necessity. Whether you are an individual protecting personal files, a business owner safeguarding client information, or simply someone who values privacy, building a strong digital defense is essential. The internet offers convenience and opportunity, but without proper security measures, it can also be a dangerous landscape filled with threats such as phishing scams, malware attacks, and data breaches.

This chapter provides a step-by-step guide to fortifying your digital presence. You will learn about essential security measures, best practices for protecting your online accounts, and tools that can help shield your personal information from cyber threats. By implementing these strategies, you can create a secure digital environment that minimizes vulnerabilities and ensures that your private data remains protected.

Understanding Digital Threats: What Are We Up Against?

Common Cyber Threats

To build an effective defense, it's crucial to understand the types of cyber threats that exist. Below are some of the most common digital threats:

- **Phishing Attacks:** Fraudulent emails or messages designed to trick users into revealing sensitive information.
- **Malware and Ransomware:** Malicious software that can infiltrate systems, steal data, or lock users out of their own devices until a ransom is paid.
- **Man-in-the-Middle Attacks (MitM):** Cybercriminals intercept communication between two parties to steal or manipulate data.
- **Data Breaches:** Unauthorized access to databases that expose personal information to hackers.

- **Credential Stuffing:** Hackers use stolen usernames and passwords to gain access to other accounts where users have reused credentials.
- **Spyware:** Software that secretly records user activity, including keystrokes and personal data.

Understanding these threats is the first step in mitigating risks and strengthening your digital security. For example, in 2021, a massive phishing campaign targeted over 50,000 businesses worldwide, tricking employees into revealing credentials that led to widespread data breaches. Such real-world incidents illustrate how crucial it is to recognize and defend against these threats proactively.

Step 1: Strengthening Your Passwords and Authentication Methods

Creating Strong, Unique Passwords

Passwords are the first line of defense in digital security. Weak or reused passwords make it easier for hackers to gain unauthorized access to your accounts. Here are key principles for strong passwords:

- Use a mix of uppercase and lowercase letters, numbers, and special characters.

- Make passwords at least 12-16 characters long.

- Avoid easily guessed words such as birthdays, names, or common phrases.

- Use passphrases—randomly combined words that are both long and difficult to crack (e.g., "Sunset$Giraffe!Tornado123").

Using a Password Manager

Managing multiple strong passwords can be challenging. A password manager, such as Bitwarden, 1Password, or LastPass, securely stores and generates complex passwords, reducing the need for memorization while increasing security.

Implementing Two-Factor Authentication (2FA)

Two-factor authentication (2FA) adds an extra layer of security by requiring a second form of verification. While SMS-based 2FA is commonly used, it is vulnerable to SIM swapping attacks, where hackers can hijack phone numbers to gain unauthorized access. A more secure alternative is using authentication apps like Google Authenticator or Authy, which generate one-time codes that are not tied to mobile networks.

- A text message or email code.
- Authentication apps like Google Authenticator or Authy.
- Biometric verification (fingerprint or facial recognition).

Enabling 2FA on important accounts significantly reduces the risk of unauthorized access.

Step 2: Securing Your Devices and Networks

Keeping Software and Devices Up to Date

Hackers often exploit outdated software with known vulnerabilities. Keep your devices secure by:

- Regularly updating operating systems and applications.
- Enabling automatic updates whenever possible.
- Installing security patches as soon as they are released.

Using a Virtual Private Network (VPN)

A VPN encrypts your internet connection, making it harder for hackers to intercept your data. It is especially useful when using public Wi-Fi networks, where security risks are higher.

Configuring a Secure Home Network

Securing your home Wi-Fi reduces the risk of cyber intrusions. Best practices include:

- Changing the default router username and password.
- Enabling WPA3 encryption for the strongest security.
- Hiding your Wi-Fi network name (SSID) to prevent unauthorized access.
- Using a separate guest network for visitors to avoid sharing access to your main devices.

Step 3: Enhancing Online Privacy and Reducing Digital Footprint

Minimizing Data Exposure on Social Media

Cybercriminals often gather information from social media to impersonate users or execute scams. Reduce your digital footprint by:

- Limiting the amount of personal information you share online.
- Adjusting privacy settings to restrict access to your data.

- Avoiding publicizing location check-ins, travel plans, and personal milestones.

Using Privacy-Focused Search Engines and Browsers

Mainstream search engines and browsers track user activity for targeted ads. Privacy-focused alternatives include:

- **Browsers:** Brave, Firefox, or Tor for enhanced privacy.
- **Search Engines:** DuckDuckGo or Startpage for private searches that do not track user data.

Opting Out of Data Collection and Removing Old Accounts

Many online services collect and store unnecessary personal data. High-profile data breaches, such as the 2019 Facebook leak that exposed over 530 million users' personal details, illustrate the dangers of companies retaining excessive user information. When these databases are compromised, the impact can range from identity theft to financial fraud, underscoring the importance of limiting data exposure. Reduce your exposure by:

- Deleting old accounts that are no longer in use.
- Reviewing and limiting app permissions.
- Using websites like JustDeleteMe to locate and remove unused accounts.

Step 4: Recognizing and Avoiding Online Scams

Spotting Phishing Attempts

Phishing emails and messages often mimic legitimate organizations to steal personal information. Key warning signs include:

- Generic greetings instead of personalized names.
- Requests for urgent action or account verification.
- Suspicious links or attachments.
- Poor grammar and formatting errors.

Verifying Requests for Information

Never provide sensitive information without verifying the authenticity of the request. Contact companies directly through official channels rather than responding to unsolicited messages.

Step 5: Maintaining Long-Term Digital Security

Conducting Regular Security Audits

Cybersecurity is not a one-time effort—it requires continuous monitoring. Perform regular security audits by:

- Checking account activity for suspicious behavior.
- Reviewing and updating passwords periodically.
- Ensuring all devices and applications remain updated.

Developing a Digital Security Routine

A strong digital defense requires consistent habits. Below is a simple checklist to help reinforce key security practices:

- **Update Software Regularly**: Ensure your operating system, apps, and security patches are up to date.
- **Use Strong, Unique Passwords**: Avoid password reuse and utilize a password manager.
- **Enable Two-Factor Authentication (2FA)**: Add an extra layer of security to all critical accounts.

- **Monitor Account Activity**: Regularly review login attempts and account activity for suspicious behavior.
- **Secure Your Home Network**: Change default router credentials and enable WPA3 encryption.
- **Limit Data Exposure**: Remove unused online accounts and minimize personal data sharing.
- **Recognize Phishing Scams**: Avoid clicking on suspicious links and verify sources before providing information.
- **Use Privacy-Focused Tools**: Consider VPNs, secure browsers, and encrypted messaging apps for better privacy protection.

By consistently practicing these habits, you can maintain a secure digital environment and reduce your vulnerability to cyber threats. Establish a security routine that includes:

- Weekly checks for software updates.
- Monthly password changes for critical accounts.
- Quarterly reviews of online privacy settings.

Conclusion: Taking Control of Your Digital Security

Building a robust digital defense is essential in today's interconnected world. Cyber threats are ever-evolving, but by understanding digital risks and implementing proactive security measures, you can significantly reduce your vulnerability to cyberattacks.

By using strong passwords, securing your devices, minimizing your digital footprint, and staying alert for online scams, you take control of your digital security and protect your personal and professional data.

In the next chapter, we will explore the best tools and apps available for enhancing your digital security and privacy, ensuring that you stay one step ahead of cyber threats. Let's continue this journey toward a more secure and private digital life.

Chapter 6

Managing Your Online Footprint

Introduction: Why Your Online Footprint Matters

Every action you take online—every search, social media post, and website visit—leaves behind a digital trace. This accumulated data forms your online footprint, a collection of publicly accessible and privately stored information that defines your digital identity. In today's world, where personal data is currency, managing your online footprint is crucial to maintaining privacy, security, and professional integrity.

Your online presence can influence job opportunities, financial transactions, and personal safety. For example, a 2020 CareerBuilder survey found that 70% of employers screen candidates' social media before making hiring decisions, with nearly half rejecting candidates due to inappropriate online content. Similarly, some financial institutions assess digital behavior when determining creditworthiness, demonstrating how an unmanaged digital footprint can impact various aspects of life. Employers conduct background checks using social media, financial institutions assess digital behavior to gauge creditworthiness, and cybercriminals exploit online information for fraud. In this chapter, we'll explore how to take control of your digital identity by reducing exposure, managing privacy settings, and securing your personal information.

Understanding Your Digital Footprint

What Is an Online Footprint?

Your online footprint consists of two primary types:

1. **Active Digital Footprint** – This includes data you deliberately share, such as social media posts, blog articles, and online reviews.
2. **Passive Digital Footprint** – This is information collected without your direct input, such as cookies tracking your browsing history, location data stored by apps, and metadata gathered by websites.

Understanding the distinction between these two can help you assess where your data is being stored and who has access to it.

How Your Data Is Collected and Stored

Many companies and third-party organizations gather user data for marketing, analytics, and surveillance purposes. Common data collection methods include:

- **Cookies and Trackers** – Websites place cookies on your device to track browsing habits and preferences.
- **Social Media Interactions** – Every comment, like, and post contributes to a growing data profile.
- **Search Engine Logs** – Search providers retain queries to refine algorithms and target advertisements.
- **Online Purchases** – Retailers track purchase history and payment details for targeted promotions.
- **Public Records and Data Brokers** – Your address, phone number, and financial history may be available from government databases and data-selling firms.

Assessing Your Online Presence

Before you can manage your footprint, you need to assess its scope. Here's how:

Step 1: Google Yourself

Performing a self-search on Google and other search engines can reveal what information is publicly accessible. For example, John, a marketing professional, once Googled himself and discovered that an outdated profile from a previous job was still appearing in search results. Additionally, he found his phone number listed on a data broker site. This prompted him to update his online profiles, remove old accounts, and request data removal from third-party sites, improving his privacy and professional image. Key aspects to look for include:

- Personal details such as phone numbers, addresses, or emails.
- Social media profiles that may be visible to the public.
- Old accounts or posts that may no longer represent your current self.
- Mentions on forums, blogs, or news articles.

Step 2: Check Data Broker Sites

Several websites compile personal data and sell it to marketers, employers, and even cybercriminals. Websites like Spokeo, Whitepages, and MyLife often have profiles on individuals. Services like **DeleteMe** or **OneRep** can help remove these listings.

Step 3: Review Social Media Exposure

Each social media platform has different privacy settings. Review and adjust:

- Profile visibility settings.
- Who can tag or mention you.
- Information shared with third-party apps.
- Past posts and shared content.

Reducing Your Digital Exposure

Limit Personal Information Sharing

Be mindful of the details you share online. Avoid:

- Posting full birthdates, home addresses, or phone numbers.
- Using personal details in usernames or passwords.
- Answering quizzes that collect data for profiling.

Deactivate or Delete Old Accounts

Dormant accounts pose security risks. To remove them:

- Use services like **JustDeleteMe** to locate and close unused accounts.
- Check email inboxes for account registration confirmation messages.
- Delete old forum and blog profiles.

Use a Privacy-Focused Email Address (e.g., ProtonMail, Tutanota)

Consider setting up separate email addresses for different purposes:

- One for banking and official matters.
- One for casual online interactions.
- A disposable email for temporary registrations.

Opt-Out of Data Collection

Many platforms allow users to limit data collection. Steps include:

- Disabling ad personalization in Google, Facebook, and Apple accounts.
- Requesting removal from data broker sites.
- Using tools like **Privacy Badger** or **uBlock Origin** to block trackers.

Enhancing Privacy on Social Media

Social media platforms often have intricate privacy settings that default to public exposure. Below is a comparison of privacy settings across major social media platforms:

Platform	Default Privacy Settings	Key Privacy Features
Facebook	Public posts by default	Restrict post visibility, limit profile searchability, disable facial recognition
Instagram	Public profile by default	Switch to private, control who can message you, disable location tagging
Twitter (X)	Public tweets by default	Protect tweets, limit who can reply, disable tracking across sites
LinkedIn	Profile visible to all	Restrict profile visibility, manage data sharing with third parties

Adjusting these settings can help you take control of your personal data and limit who has access to your online information. Adjusting these can help you take control of your personal data.

Review Your Privacy Settings

Each platform provides options to limit data sharing:

- **Facebook:** Restrict who can see your posts and profile details.
- **Instagram:** Switch to a private account to control follower access.
- **Twitter (X):** Enable protected tweets to limit exposure.
- **LinkedIn:** Adjust visibility for connections and profile searches.

Delete Old Posts and Media

Some platforms, like Facebook, allow bulk deletion of past posts. Manually review and remove outdated content or use **TweetDelete** for clearing Twitter history.

Limit Third-Party App Access

Check which apps are connected to your accounts and remove unnecessary integrations that might collect personal data.

Strengthening Security to Protect Your Online Identity

Use Strong Passwords and 2FA

A compromised password can expose multiple accounts. Best practices include:

- Using unique passwords for each platform.
- Enabling **two-factor authentication (2FA)** wherever possible.
- Using a password manager for secure storage.

Secure Your Devices

Online footprint management extends beyond social media. Ensure:

- Your phone and laptop use strong passwords or biometric locks.
- You log out of accounts when using shared devices.
- Your browsing data is cleared regularly.

Use a VPN and Secure Browsers

Virtual Private Networks (VPNs) encrypt data, preventing surveillance and tracking. Recommended browsers include:

- **Brave** – Blocks ads and trackers by default.
- **Firefox** – Enhanced security features for private browsing.
- **Tor** – Best for complete anonymity.

Long-Term Strategies for a Minimal Online Footprint

Maintaining a reduced digital footprint is an ongoing process. Here's a quick checklist to help you stay on top of your online privacy:

- **Conduct Regular Self-Audits:** Google yourself every few months to check what information is publicly available.
- **Review and Update Privacy Settings:** Adjust privacy settings on social media and online accounts periodically.
- **Delete or Deactivate Old Accounts:** Close accounts you no longer use to minimize data exposure.
- **Use Privacy-Focused Tools:** Opt for secure email providers, VPNs, and privacy-focused browsers.
- **Limit Data Sharing:** Be mindful of the personal information you share online and opt out of data collection when possible.
- **Monitor Third-Party App Permissions:** Regularly check which apps have access to your data and revoke unnecessary permissions.

- **Stay Informed:** Keep up with the latest cybersecurity threats and best practices to maintain a strong digital defense.

By consistently following these steps, you can take control of your digital footprint and ensure your personal data remains protected. Consider:

- **Regular Self-Audits:** Check search engine results and privacy settings every few months.
- **Minimalist Online Engagement:** Use pseudonyms for non-essential online activity.
- **Secure Digital Legacy Planning:** Set up instructions for your accounts in case of incapacitation.

Conclusion: Taking Back Control of Your Online Presence

Your online footprint is a reflection of your digital identity. Without proper management, personal data can be misused or exploited. By auditing your presence, limiting exposure, and enhancing privacy settings, you regain control over your digital narrative.

In the next chapter, we will explore **digital tools and apps** that can further enhance privacy and security, providing practical solutions to keep your information safe from prying eyes. Let's take the next step toward a safer and more intentional online presence.

Chapter 7

Essential Tools and Apps for a Minimalist and Secure Digital Life

Introduction: Equipping Yourself for a Safer Digital Experience

In an age where digital threats are constantly evolving and our online lives are becoming increasingly cluttered, having the right tools is crucial. Whether you want to minimize distractions, protect your privacy, or enhance your cybersecurity, leveraging the right apps and software can transform your digital experience.

This chapter provides a comprehensive overview of the best tools and applications that help you maintain a minimalist, secure, and efficient digital life. Imagine Sarah, a freelance writer who struggled with password fatigue, overwhelming email clutter, and constant online tracking. By switching to a password manager, using a privacy-focused email provider, and enabling a VPN, she streamlined her workflow while significantly enhancing her online security. These tools not only reduced her digital clutter but also protected her from potential data breaches, demonstrating how small changes can have a profound impact on digital well-being. From password managers to privacy-focused search engines, you'll find expert-recommended solutions that align with the principles of digital minimalism and data security.

Password Management and Authentication Tools

Why Strong Passwords Are Non-Negotiable

Passwords are the first line of defense against cyber threats. Weak passwords or reusing the same password across multiple accounts make you vulnerable to breaches. To create and manage strong passwords effectively, consider using a dedicated password manager.

Recommended Password Managers

- **Bitwarden** – An open-source, end-to-end encrypted password manager with cross-device sync.
- **1Password** – A highly secure and feature-rich password manager with encrypted vaults.
- **LastPass** – Offers free and premium options, providing encrypted storage and multi-device access.
- **NordPass** – Developed by the creators of NordVPN, featuring strong encryption and biometric login support.

Two-Factor Authentication (2FA) Apps

Two-factor authentication (2FA) adds an extra security layer beyond your password. Instead of relying on SMS codes, which can be intercepted, use dedicated authentication apps:

- **Authy** – Offers cloud backup and multi-device sync for your 2FA codes.
- **Google Authenticator** – A simple, widely-used authentication tool for securing accounts.
- **Microsoft Authenticator** – Provides both 2FA codes and password-free login options.

Secure Browsing and Private Search Engines

Why Your Choice of Browser Matters

Many mainstream browsers track user data and serve targeted ads. Privacy-focused browsers limit tracking, enhance security, and improve online anonymity.

Recommended Privacy-Focused Browsers

- **Brave** – Blocks ads, trackers, and fingerprinting by default while offering a fast browsing experience.
- **Mozilla Firefox** – Customizable privacy settings and an open-source framework that prioritizes user security.

- **Tor Browser** – Uses the Tor network to anonymize browsing and prevent tracking.

Private Search Engines

Mainstream search engines like Google collect massive amounts of user data. A 2022 study by Surfshark found that Google collects 39 types of personal data, including location history, search queries, and app usage, making it one of the most invasive search engines in terms of user tracking. Switching to a privacy-first search engine prevents tracking and improves anonymity.

- **DuckDuckGo** – Doesn't store search history and blocks trackers.
- **Startpage** – Provides Google search results without tracking users.
- **Mojeek** – An independent search engine that does not track or personalize search results.

Virtual Private Networks (VPNs) and Encrypted Communication

The Role of VPNs in Digital Privacy

A Virtual Private Network (VPN) encrypts your internet connection, preventing ISPs, advertisers, and cybercriminals from tracking your online activity.

Top VPN Services

- **ProtonVPN** – No-logs policy, strong encryption, and a free plan with unlimited bandwidth.
- **NordVPN** – Features double VPN encryption and advanced security protocols.
- **ExpressVPN** – Known for fast speeds and excellent security across all platforms.
- **Mullvad VPN** – Prioritizes anonymity with cash payments and no user logs.

Encrypted Messaging Apps

Standard messaging apps often lack strong privacy protections. For truly secure conversations, use:

- **Signal** – End-to-end encrypted messaging with open-source transparency.
- **Telegram (Secret Chats)** – Encrypted chats with self-destructing messages.
- **Session** – A decentralized, anonymous messaging platform with no metadata storage.

Cloud Storage and Secure File-Sharing

Privacy-First Cloud Storage Providers

Instead of mainstream cloud providers like Google Drive or Dropbox, which can access and scan your files, opt for privacy-focused alternatives. Below is a comparison of mainstream and privacy-focused cloud services:

Feature	Google Drive / Dropbox	Proton Drive / Sync.com / Tresorit
Data Encryption	Encrypted, but provider can access files	Zero-knowledge encryption (only user has access)
Privacy Policies	Data may be shared with third parties	No data sharing, strict privacy policies
Open-Source	Proprietary code	Some providers offer open-source transparency
Security Breaches	History of past data breaches	No major breaches reported

Choosing a privacy-focused cloud provider ensures your files remain secure and inaccessible to third parties.

- **Proton Drive** – Encrypted cloud storage from the makers of ProtonMail.
- **Sync.com** – Zero-knowledge encryption, ensuring only you can access your data.

- **Tresorit** – Enterprise-grade security with zero-trust architecture.

Secure File-Sharing Tools

- **Firefox Send** (Discontinued but alternative self-hosted versions exist) – Encrypted, temporary file-sharing.
- **OnionShare** – Share files over the Tor network securely and anonymously.
- **SendGB** – No-registration, encrypted file transfers up to 5GB.

Blocking Trackers and Digital Clutter Reduction

Ad and Tracker Blockers

To reduce digital distractions and prevent companies from tracking your behavior:

- **uBlock Origin** – Lightweight, open-source ad and tracker blocker.
- **Privacy Badger** – Automatically learns and blocks tracking scripts.
- **AdGuard** – Blocks ads system-wide across all apps and browsers.

Decluttering Digital Life

- **Joplin** – Open-source note-taking app with end-to-end encryption.
- **Standard Notes** – Secure, encrypted notes for privacy-conscious users.
- **TidyTabs** – Organizes and declutters open windows for better productivity.

Email Privacy and Disposable Email Services

Secure Email Providers

If you need an email provider that respects privacy and security:

- **ProtonMail** – End-to-end encrypted email service based in Switzerland.
- **Tutanota** – Encrypted email with zero-ads and open-source infrastructure.
- **Mailfence** – Focuses on privacy, offering encrypted email and calendar services.

Disposable Email Services

For temporary sign-ups, avoiding spam, or testing services, use:

- **Guerrilla Mail** – No registration required, disposable email service.
- **Temp Mail** – Generates temporary email addresses instantly.
- **10 Minute Mail** – Self-destructing email addresses for short-term use.

Conclusion: Building a Privacy-Focused Digital Ecosystem

By incorporating the right tools, you can enhance your digital privacy, security, and efficiency while embracing a minimalist digital lifestyle. Below is a summary table outlining key tools and their functions:

Category	Recommended Tools	Function
Password Management	Bitwarden, 1Password, LastPass, NordPass	Securely store and generate strong passwords
Two-Factor Authentication (2FA)	Authy, Google Authenticator, Microsoft Authenticator	Adds an extra layer of security to account

Private Search Engines	DuckDuckGo, Startpage, Mojeek	Prevents tracking and improves anonymity
VPN Services	ProtonVPN, NordVPN, ExpressVPN, Mullvad	Encrypts internet traffic for secure browsing
Encrypted Messaging	Signal, Telegram (Secret Chats), Session	Ensures private and secure communications
Cloud Storage	Proton Drive, Sync.com, Tresorit	Encrypted storage to protect sensitive files
Ad & Tracker Blockers	uBlock Origin, Privacy Badger, AdGuard	Blocks ads and tracking scripts for better privacy
Secure Email Providers	ProtonMail, Tutanota, Mailfence	Provides encrypted and privacy-focused email services

Using these tools consistently will help build a strong digital defense while simplifying your online experience. Password managers, private search engines, encrypted communication apps, and secure cloud storage solutions provide the foundation for a safer online experience.

In the next chapter, we'll discuss **how to create lasting digital habits** that reinforce your minimalist and secure approach to technology, ensuring that your efforts remain effective over the long term.

Chapter 8

Developing Sustainable Digital Habits

Introduction: The Importance of Digital Discipline

The modern world is a digital landscape, filled with opportunities and distractions alike. While technology has undoubtedly enhanced our lives, it has also led to an overreliance on digital devices, affecting productivity, mental health, and overall well-being. Developing sustainable digital habits is not about rejecting technology—it's about using it intentionally, in a way that aligns with our values and goals.

In this chapter, we'll explore how to create lasting digital habits that enhance efficiency, security, and personal growth. From mindful screen time management to structured digital detoxes, these strategies will empower you to take control of your digital environment and maintain a balanced, sustainable relationship with technology.

Understanding Digital Overload

The Psychology Behind Digital Addiction

The pull of digital platforms is no accident—tech companies design apps and websites to capture attention for as long as possible. Understanding the psychological mechanisms behind digital addiction can help us counteract them. For example, studies have shown that individuals who receive frequent notifications from social media apps often experience increased anxiety and compulsive phone-checking behaviors. A case study involving a college student named Jake found that disabling non-essential notifications and implementing scheduled screen breaks significantly reduced his stress levels and improved his focus on studies. This illustrates how small adjustments can counteract the addictive nature of digital platforms.

- **The Dopamine Loop:** Every notification, like, or message triggers a small dopamine release, reinforcing compulsive checking behavior.
- **Infinite Scroll and Autoplay:** Social media and video platforms keep users engaged with endless content loops.
- **Fear of Missing Out (FOMO):** Social pressure and real-time updates create anxiety around staying connected.

The Consequences of Digital Overload

Excessive screen time can impact multiple areas of life, including:

- **Mental Health:** Increased anxiety, depression, and decreased focus.
- **Productivity:** Constant interruptions reduce deep work and cognitive efficiency.
- **Physical Health:** Eye strain, poor posture, and sleep disruption.

Recognizing these effects is the first step toward reclaiming control over digital consumption.

Building Healthy Digital Habits

1. Practicing Mindful Technology Use

To develop sustainable digital habits, approach technology with intention rather than impulse.

- **Set Clear Goals:** Define why and how you use each digital tool.
- **Time Blocking:** Allocate specific periods for checking emails, social media, and leisure browsing.
- **Single-Tasking Over Multitasking:** Focus on one digital activity at a time to improve efficiency and engagement.

2. Implementing a Screen Time Budget

Monitoring and controlling screen time prevents overuse and fosters balance.

- **Track Usage:** Apps like RescueTime and Apple's Screen Time provide insights into daily device usage.
- **Set Limits:** Restrict access to non-essential apps during work hours.
- **Establish No-Tech Zones:** Keep certain spaces (e.g., bedroom, dining area) free from digital distractions.

3. Digital Detox Strategies

Periodic breaks from technology allow for mental and emotional reset. Consider implementing a structured detox schedule to maintain balance:

Detox Type	Duration	Suggested Activities
Daily Mini-Detox	30-60 minutes	Walks, meditation, reading
Weekend Detox	1 full day	Outdoor activities, social gatherings

Extended Detox   7-30 days   Travel, deep work, personal projects

By incorporating these structured breaks into your routine, you can reduce stress, improve focus, and foster a healthier relationship with technology.

- **Daily Mini-Detoxes:** Set aside 30-60 minutes daily for screen-free activities.
- **Weekend Detoxes:** Designate one day a week for reduced screen time.
- **Extended Detox Challenges:** Take a 7-day or 30-day digital detox to reassess long-term digital habits.

Optimizing Digital Workflows

1. Decluttering Your Digital Space

A cluttered digital environment mirrors a cluttered mind. Organizing digital files, emails, and apps improves efficiency and reduces stress.

- **Inbox Zero:** Maintain an organized email inbox with filters, folders, and scheduled cleanups.
- **App Minimalism:** Keep only essential apps to avoid distractions.

- **File Organization:** Structure digital documents with a logical naming system and cloud backups.

2. Using Productivity-Enhancing Tools

Leverage digital tools to enhance focus rather than contribute to distractions. Below is a comparison of distraction-heavy apps versus productivity-enhancing alternatives:

Category	Distraction-Heavy Apps	Productivity-Enhancing Tools
Social Media	Instagram, TikTok, Facebook	Feedless, Minimalist Twitter, Focus Mode
Video Streaming	YouTube, Netflix autoplay	Pocket, Matter (save videos for later)
Email Management	Gmail without filters	Superhuman, Hey Email (prioritized inbox)
Task Management	Basic Notes Apps	Notion, Todoist, Trello

| Browsing | Chrome with no restrictions | Brave, Firefox with uBlock Origin |

By consciously selecting tools that minimize distractions, you can create a more efficient and focused digital environment.

- **Focus Apps:** Tools like Forest and Freedom block distractions during work sessions.
- **Task Management:** Notion, Todoist, and Trello help streamline workflows and task prioritization.
- **Automation Tools:** Zapier and IFTTT automate repetitive digital tasks, freeing up mental bandwidth.

Protecting Your Digital Well-Being

1. Managing Digital Boundaries

Healthy digital boundaries prevent technology from interfering with personal relationships and mental well-being.

- **Notification Control:** Disable non-essential notifications to reduce interruptions.
- **Work-Life Separation:** Avoid checking work emails outside of designated hours.

- **Social Media Mindfulness:** Unfollow accounts that don't add value and limit engagement in online debates.

2. Prioritizing Digital Security

Sustainable digital habits include safeguarding personal data and online privacy.

- **Use Strong Passwords & 2FA:** Implement password managers and two-factor authentication for all accounts.
- **Regular Security Audits:** Periodically check and update privacy settings on apps and websites.
- **Be Cautious with Public Wi-Fi:** Always use a VPN when accessing sensitive data on public networks.

Developing a Long-Term Digital Wellness Plan

Creating sustainable digital habits requires long-term commitment and adaptability.

1. Conduct Regular Digital Check-Ins

Periodically assessing digital habits ensures they align with personal goals.

- **Monthly Reviews:** Evaluate screen time reports and adjust habits accordingly.
- **Annual Digital Reset:** Take a step back yearly to reassess technology's role in your life.
- **Mindful Reflection:** Ask, "Is my technology use enhancing or hindering my well-being?"

2. Creating a Personalized Digital Minimalism Framework

A one-size-fits-all approach doesn't work for digital well-being—tailor a plan that aligns with your values.

- **Essentialism:** Identify which digital tools truly add value to your life.
- **Scheduled Digital Downtime:** Set intentional unplugged hours based on lifestyle needs.
- **Accountability Partnerships:** Engage with friends or family members to stay committed to healthier digital habits.

Conclusion: Embracing a Balanced Digital Life

Sustainable digital habits are not about eliminating technology but about using it intentionally and mindfully. Key takeaways from this chapter include:

- **Mindful Technology Use:** Approach digital tools with purpose rather than impulse.
- **Digital Detox Strategies:** Implement structured screen breaks to maintain balance.
- **Optimized Workflows:** Use productivity-enhancing tools to minimize digital clutter.
- **Digital Boundaries:** Set clear limits on social media, work emails, and notifications.
- **Security Best Practices:** Regularly update passwords, use 2FA, and secure personal data.
- **Long-Term Digital Wellness:** Periodically review habits and adjust them to align with personal goals.

By integrating these strategies, you can cultivate a healthier, more intentional relationship with technology. By setting boundaries, optimizing workflows, and prioritizing digital well-being, you can reclaim control over your digital life while maintaining security and efficiency.

The next chapter will explore how to apply these principles to different areas of life, from work and education to relationships and leisure, ensuring that your digital habits continue to support—not hinder—your overall well-being.

Chapter 9

Looking Ahead: The Future of Digital Wellbeing

Introduction: The Evolving Landscape of Digital Wellbeing

Technology continues to shape how we live, work, and interact. As digital tools become more embedded in everyday life, the need for conscious, well-balanced engagement with technology has never been greater. Digital wellbeing is not a static concept—it evolves alongside advancements in artificial intelligence, virtual reality, and data privacy regulations. Looking ahead, we must examine the trends, challenges, and opportunities that will influence the future of digital wellbeing. These factors will redefine how we maintain a balanced and healthy relationship with technology in an increasingly digital world.

This chapter explores emerging innovations, potential risks, and proactive strategies for ensuring digital wellbeing in an increasingly connected world.

The Role of Artificial Intelligence in Digital Wellbeing

1. AI-Powered Personal Assistants for Wellbeing

Artificial Intelligence (AI) is revolutionizing digital wellness by creating personalized experiences that help individuals maintain healthier digital habits. AI-driven applications are now capable of:

- Monitoring screen time and recommending mindful breaks.
- Customizing digital detox plans based on individual behavior.
- Filtering content to reduce exposure to harmful or distressing material.

Examples include Google's Digital Wellbeing tools, Apple's Screen Time analytics, and AI-driven mindfulness apps like Calm and Headspace.

2. AI and Ethical Concerns

While AI offers great potential for enhancing digital wellbeing, it also presents ethical concerns, including: For example, AI-powered recommendation algorithms on social media platforms have been found to reinforce echo chambers and spread misinformation. In 2021, Facebook's internal research revealed that its algorithm sometimes prioritized engagement over accuracy, amplifying misleading content. Such instances highlight the need for transparency and responsible AI development in digital wellbeing initiatives.

- The risk of excessive personalization leading to digital echo chambers.
- Privacy concerns regarding AI tracking and data collection.
- Algorithmic bias influencing content exposure and decision-making.

As AI becomes more integrated into digital experiences, balancing convenience with ethical responsibility will be critical.

The Rise of Digital Minimalism in an AI-Driven World

1. The Movement Toward Intentional Technology Use

Digital minimalism, a movement emphasizing the mindful and intentional use of technology, is gaining traction. The future will likely see an increase in:

- The adoption of distraction-free smartphones and apps.
- Greater consumer demand for digital decluttering tools.
- Companies prioritizing user wellbeing by offering more control over notifications and content consumption.

2. The Role of Tech Companies in Promoting Digital Wellbeing

As awareness of digital wellbeing grows, major technology firms are beginning to integrate wellness-focused features, including:

- Social media platforms adding screen time reminders and focus modes.
- Streaming services allowing users to limit autoplay and binge-watching.
- Workplace productivity tools offering digital wellness insights to balance work-life integration.

However, the challenge remains in ensuring these features are effective and not merely marketing strategies.

The Future of Privacy and Digital Autonomy

1. Data Privacy Regulations and User Empowerment

As concerns over data privacy continue to rise, future developments may include:

- Stricter global regulations governing how companies collect and use personal data.
- Decentralized platforms that prioritize user control and data ownership.

- Increased adoption of blockchain technology to enhance data security and transparency.

2. The Shift Toward Decentralized Internet

A major shift in digital autonomy may arise with Web3 and decentralized applications (dApps), which represent a new phase of the internet focused on decentralization and user control. Unlike traditional web platforms that rely on centralized entities like Google or Facebook to manage data, Web3 operates on blockchain technology, enabling users to interact directly without intermediaries. For example, platforms like Mastodon provide a decentralized social networking alternative to Twitter, giving users control over their data and reducing corporate influence over online discourse.

- Reduce reliance on centralized corporations controlling data.
- Allow users to retain full ownership over digital assets and content.
- Foster a more transparent and ethical internet ecosystem.

However, challenges such as accessibility, usability, and regulation of decentralized platforms must be addressed.

The Role of Virtual and Augmented Reality in Digital Wellbeing

1. The Benefits and Risks of Immersive Technology

Virtual Reality (VR) and Augmented Reality (AR) are transforming entertainment, education, and professional environments. Benefits include:

- VR-based therapy programs improving mental health outcomes.
- AR tools aiding focus by reducing workplace distractions.
- Gamified mindfulness apps creating immersive relaxation experiences.

However, prolonged use of immersive technologies can lead to: A 2021 study by Stanford University found that excessive VR use can contribute to 'Zoom fatigue' symptoms, including increased eye strain, cognitive overload, and social disconnection. For instance, users engaging in extended VR gaming sessions have reported difficulties readjusting to real-world interactions, highlighting concerns over digital escapism and dependency. These findings underscore the importance of setting limits on immersive technology use to maintain a balanced digital life.

- Increased screen time and digital escapism.
- Ethical concerns about deepfake content and digital manipulation.
- Potential cognitive overload from hyperrealistic environments.

2. Future Solutions for Balancing VR/AR Usage

To mitigate risks, future trends may include:

- Built-in digital wellness features within VR/AR platforms.
- Stricter regulation on ethical content creation in virtual environments.
- AI-driven personalized guidelines to help users maintain healthy screen time habits.

Next-Generation Tools for Digital Wellbeing

1. Advanced Digital Wellbeing Apps

The future will see smarter applications designed to proactively assist users in managing screen time, minimizing distractions, and improving productivity.

Emerging trends include:

- AI-driven wellness bots that provide real-time behavior feedback.

- Adaptive digital detox plans based on user engagement patterns.
- Mindful notifications that prioritize important alerts while reducing noise.

2. Biometric Feedback for Wellbeing

Wearable technology is advancing to include:

- Real-time stress monitoring through biometric sensors.
- AI-driven recommendations for reducing digital burnout.
- Haptic feedback devices that provide non-intrusive reminders for breaks and movement.

These innovations will help individuals develop healthier relationships with technology by making them more aware of their physical and mental responses to digital interactions.

Creating a Future-Proof Digital Wellbeing Strategy

1. Building a Sustainable Digital Lifestyle

To ensure long-term digital wellbeing, individuals can adopt proactive habits such as:

- Setting clear boundaries for digital consumption.
- Practicing regular digital detoxes and screen-free time.
- Choosing ethical technology providers that prioritize privacy and user wellbeing.

2. Encouraging Digital Literacy and Awareness

Educational initiatives will play a crucial role in shaping the future of digital wellbeing. Below is a summary of key digital literacy programs that are shaping this future:

Initiative	Focus Area	Impact
School Digital Literacy Programs	Teaching students about online privacy, responsible social media use, and cybersecurity	Helps young users develop responsible digital habits early on
Corporate Digital Wellness Programs	Training employees on work-life balance, reducing screen fatigue, and secure online practices	Enhances productivity and mental well-being in the workplace

Public Awareness Campaigns	Government and nonprofit-led initiatives to educate the public on digital safety and privacy	Raises awareness about data protection and online risks
Policy Advocacy for Digital Rights	Pushing for stricter regulations on data collection, AI ethics, and online consumer rights	Ensures better privacy protections and fair digital practices

These initiatives highlight the growing commitment to fostering a healthier and more secure digital landscape for individuals worldwide. Key developments may include:

- Schools incorporating digital wellness into curricula.
- Employers providing digital health programs for work-life balance.
- Advocacy for policies that promote responsible technology use in society.

Conclusion: Preparing for the Future of Digital Wellbeing

The future of digital wellbeing is being shaped by advancements in AI, privacy regulations, digital minimalism, and immersive technology. As we move forward, individuals, companies, and policymakers must collaborate to create a digital ecosystem that fosters intentional use, security, and personal empowerment.

By staying informed and adopting proactive digital habits, we can embrace a future where technology enhances, rather than hinders, our well-being. In the final chapter, we will explore actionable strategies for applying digital wellbeing principles to different aspects of life, ensuring a balanced and sustainable approach to the digital age.

Conclusion

Your Path Forward

Embrace a Simplified, Secure Digital Life

Introduction: A New Digital Beginning

Throughout this journey, we have explored the evolving landscape of digital wellbeing, the tools to create a balanced and secure digital life, and strategies to maintain long-term mindfulness in our technological interactions. The digital world will continue to evolve, and with it, so must our approach to engaging with technology. The path forward is not about abandoning technology but about embracing it with intentionality, security, and simplicity. By prioritizing mindful digital habits, leveraging tools that enhance efficiency rather than distraction, and maintaining a strong commitment to privacy, you can create a digital environment that supports, rather than hinders, your goals.

This concluding chapter provides a roadmap for sustaining the principles discussed in this book, ensuring that your digital habits align with your personal and professional goals. By implementing the right strategies and maintaining vigilance, you can lead a digitally secure, distraction-free, and fulfilling life.

Refining Your Digital Minimalism Approach

1. The Key to Intentional Technology Use

Digital minimalism is a lifestyle, not a one-time fix. To continue fostering a mindful approach to technology, remember:

- **Audit Your Digital Habits Regularly** – Set monthly or quarterly check-ins to assess whether your technology use aligns with your goals.
- **Define Core Digital Priorities** – Identify which digital tools genuinely add value and remove those that create unnecessary clutter.
- **Embrace the 80/20 Rule** – Apply the Pareto Principle to your digital life by focusing on the 20% of digital tools and platforms that provide 80% of the benefits.

2. Maintaining a Clutter-Free Digital Space

Over time, digital clutter accumulates. Adopt an ongoing maintenance plan with these key strategies:

Strategy	Action Steps
Schedule Digital Decluttering Sessions	Conduct weekly or monthly cleanups to remove unnecessary files, emails, and apps.
Practice App Minimalism	Keep only essential apps on your devices to reduce distractions and improve performance.
Limit Subscriptions	Regularly review and cancel unused digital services to avoid accumulating unnecessary expenses and distractions.
Organize Cloud Storage	Structure files in cloud platforms efficiently, deleting redundant data to keep storage streamlined.
Manage Notifications	Disable non-essential notifications to prevent digital overload and maintain focus.

By integrating these habits into your routine, you can maintain a clutter-free and efficient digital environment.

- **Schedule Digital Decluttering Sessions** – Weekly or monthly cleanups prevent unnecessary data accumulation.
- **Practice App Minimalism** – Keep only essential apps on your devices to reduce distractions.
- **Limit Subscriptions** – Cancel unused digital services that no longer serve a purpose.

Sustaining Digital Security and Privacy

1. The Importance of Cyber Hygiene

Security threats evolve, making it essential to establish routine cybersecurity practices:

- **Update Passwords and Use 2FA** – Rotate passwords every few months and enable two-factor authentication for critical accounts.
- **Conduct Security Audits** – Check for unauthorized logins, privacy settings, and outdated security practices.
- **Limit Data Sharing** – Be mindful of the personal information you share with companies and online platforms.

2. The Future of Digital Privacy

As privacy concerns continue to grow, proactive steps ensure long-term data protection:

- **Adopt Privacy-Focused Tools** – Use privacy-conscious browsers, email providers, and search engines.
- **Opt for Decentralized Platforms** – Engage with decentralized applications (dApps) that prioritize user control over data.
- **Stay Informed on Privacy Laws** – Keep track of evolving data regulations to understand your rights and digital protections.

Balancing Work, Leisure, and Screen Time

1. Establishing Healthy Digital Boundaries

Creating a sustainable digital lifestyle means ensuring a balance between work and personal life. For example, Sarah, a freelance graphic designer, struggled with maintaining clear boundaries between work and personal time. She found herself checking emails late at night and feeling constantly tethered to her devices. To address this, she implemented tech-free zones in her home, set strict work hours, and scheduled regular outdoor breaks. Over time, Sarah noticed a significant improvement in her mental well-being and productivity, demonstrating the power of intentional digital boundaries.

- **Implement Tech-Free Zones** – Keep devices out of bedrooms and dining areas to foster face-to-face interactions.
- **Define Work Hours Clearly** – Avoid checking work emails or messages outside of designated hours.
- **Prioritize Analog Activities** – Reading books, engaging in outdoor activities, and socializing without screens improve overall well-being.

2. Using Technology as an Enabler, Not a Distraction

Technology should serve as a tool for growth rather than a source of mindless consumption:

- **Use Productivity-Enhancing Apps** – Leverage Notion, Trello, or Focus Keeper to streamline work.
- **Automate Digital Workflows** – Set up automation for repetitive tasks using tools like Zapier.
- **Engage in Meaningful Digital Consumption** – Prioritize educational and inspiring content over endless social media scrolling.

Fostering a Long-Term Digital Wellbeing Mindset

1. Continuous Learning and Adaptation

Staying ahead in the digital world requires ongoing awareness:

- **Follow Digital Wellbeing Thought Leaders** – Stay updated with insights from experts in minimalism, cybersecurity, and productivity.
- **Experiment with Digital Detox Strategies** – Adapt detox methods to changing needs and circumstances.
- **Regularly Review Your Progress** – Reflect on how your digital habits evolve and adjust strategies accordingly.

2. Encouraging a Culture of Digital Wellbeing

Encouraging others to adopt healthier digital habits contributes to a more mindful society. For example, a recent initiative by a small business saw remarkable results when leadership implemented digital wellbeing policies. By setting device-free meeting times and encouraging employees to use focus apps, productivity increased by 20%, and reported workplace stress dropped significantly. This case study highlights how small changes can create a ripple effect, inspiring broader adoption of mindful technology use in both personal and professional environments.

- **Share Digital Wellbeing Knowledge** – Discuss security and minimalism practices with friends and family.
- **Lead by Example** – Inspire others through personal digital discipline.
- **Advocate for Ethical Tech Use** – Support ethical technology companies and policies that promote user wellbeing.

Final Thoughts: Your Digital Life, Your Control

The future of your digital wellbeing is in your hands. By embracing a minimalist approach, prioritizing security, and using technology intentionally, you are setting the foundation for a sustainable and fulfilling digital experience.

As the digital landscape evolves, so will your approach to it. The key to lasting digital wellbeing is adaptability, awareness, and an ongoing commitment to aligning technology with your values. Here's a summary of the key lessons from this book:

- **Intentional Technology Use** – Engage with technology mindfully rather than habitually.
- **Digital Minimalism** – Reduce digital clutter and prioritize tools that add real value.
- **Cybersecurity Best Practices** – Use strong passwords, two-factor authentication, and privacy-conscious tools.
- **Healthy Digital Boundaries** – Set limits on screen time, social media, and work-related digital interactions.
- **Regular Digital Detoxes** – Take breaks from technology to refresh focus and well-being.
- **Continuous Learning** – Stay informed about digital trends, privacy laws, and evolving security threats.
- **Encouraging a Digital Wellbeing Culture** – Share knowledge and inspire others to adopt healthier digital habits.

By integrating these principles into your daily life, you can maintain a simplified, secure, and balanced digital presence that aligns with your personal and professional goals.

This book has equipped you with the knowledge and tools to reclaim control over your digital life. The next step is yours to take—start today, and move forward with confidence into a balanced, secure, and simplified digital future.

Appendices

Appendix A: Digital Wellbeing Resources

1. Recommended Books on Digital Minimalism and Security

- *Digital Minimalism* by Cal Newport – A foundational guide to reclaiming focus in a world of distractions.
- *The Art of Invisibility* by Kevin Mitnick – A detailed look into personal cybersecurity and online privacy.
- *Indistractable* by Nir Eyal – A deep dive into staying focused in an age of constant digital distractions.
- *Deep Work* by Cal Newport – A powerful approach to developing better concentration in a distracted world.

2. Must-Use Digital Wellbeing Apps and Tools

- **RescueTime** – Tracks your screen time and helps improve productivity.
- **Freedom** – Blocks distracting websites and apps to enhance focus.
- **1Password/Bitwarden** – Password managers to improve online security.

- **ProtonMail** – A privacy-focused encrypted email service.
- **Brave Browser** – A privacy-oriented web browser that blocks ads and trackers.
- **Forest** – Encourages staying off your phone by growing virtual trees during focus sessions.
- **Unroll.me** – Helps manage and declutter email inboxes efficiently.
- **Privacy Badger** – A browser extension that blocks trackers and enhances privacy.

3. Websites and Online Communities

- **r/DigitalMinimalism (Reddit)** – A community discussing digital minimalism practices.
- **The Center for Humane Technology** – An organization dedicated to aligning technology with humanity's best interests.
- **EFF (Electronic Frontier Foundation)** – A nonprofit advocating for digital privacy and rights.
- **Mozilla Privacy Hub** – A resource for digital security and privacy best practices.

Appendix B: Digital Decluttering Checklist

1. Weekly Tasks

- Clear unnecessary files and downloads from your desktop.
- Empty the trash/recycle bin on all devices.
- Unsubscribe from unwanted email newsletters.
- Turn off non-essential notifications on your phone and laptop.

2. Monthly Tasks

- Review app permissions and revoke access for apps you no longer use.
- Check your digital subscriptions and cancel those that no longer serve you.
- Organize your cloud storage and delete redundant files.
- Run a cybersecurity scan for malware and update your passwords if necessary.

3. Annual Tasks

- Audit your social media presence and delete old, unnecessary posts.
- Backup important files to an external hard drive or a secure cloud service.

- Review financial accounts for any unauthorized or unnecessary subscriptions.
- Update security settings on all accounts and enable two-factor authentication.

Appendix C: Data Privacy and Security Best Practices

1. Creating Strong Passwords and Managing Them

- Use a password manager like LastPass or Bitwarden.
- Create passwords with at least 12-16 characters including numbers, symbols, and upper/lowercase letters.
- Avoid reusing passwords across multiple accounts.
- Use passphrases instead of simple words (e.g., "Sunset!Blue42$Morning").

2. Safe Browsing Habits

- Always use HTTPS-secured websites.
- Regularly clear cookies and cache from your browser.
- Use privacy-focused search engines like DuckDuckGo.

- Install browser extensions like uBlock Origin to block intrusive ads and trackers.

3. Protecting Your Personal Information Online

- Limit the amount of personal data you share on social media.
- Adjust privacy settings on social media to restrict who can see your posts.
- Regularly monitor credit reports and accounts for unusual activity.
- Use a VPN when accessing public Wi-Fi to encrypt your internet connection.

Appendix D: Digital Detox Strategies

1. Short-Term Detox (Daily & Weekly Practices)

- Implement a "no-phone hour" each morning and evening.
- Designate phone-free zones in your home (e.g., bedroom, dining table).
- Use grayscale mode on your phone to make it less visually engaging.
- Schedule specific times for checking emails and social media.

2. Medium-Term Detox (One-Week Challenges)

- Take a break from a specific platform (e.g., a week without Instagram or Twitter).
- Try a week of using your phone only for essential tasks (calls, navigation, work apps).
- Use a physical alarm clock instead of your phone.

3. Long-Term Digital Wellness Strategies

- Develop a "low-information diet" by reducing consumption of non-essential news and content.
- Schedule full tech-free weekends once a month.
- Maintain a simplified digital ecosystem by limiting the number of apps and devices you use.
- Create a system where you engage with technology only when it serves a clear purpose.

Appendix E: Work-Life Digital Balance Guide

1. Setting Boundaries in a Digital World

- Establish "office hours" for when you are available for work-related communications.
- Turn off work notifications outside of working hours.
- Use separate work and personal devices when possible.

2. Productivity Strategies for Digital Wellbeing

- Use the Pomodoro Technique (25 minutes of work, 5-minute break cycles).
- Set clear daily digital intentions before starting work.
- Utilize "Do Not Disturb" modes to enhance focus during work sessions.

3. Reducing Screen Time and Digital Fatigue

- Follow the 20-20-20 rule (every 20 minutes, look at something 20 feet away for 20 seconds).
- Invest in blue light filtering glasses or use night mode on screens.
- Incorporate offline hobbies and activities to reduce dependence on digital entertainment.

Appendix F: Emergency Digital Preparedness

1. Creating a Digital Emergency Kit

- A physical notebook with critical login credentials (securely stored).
- Backup copies of important documents on a USB drive or encrypted cloud storage.
- Contact information for banks, family, and emergency services.

- A hard-copy list of critical online accounts and recovery options.

2. What to Do in Case of a Security Breach

- Immediately change compromised passwords.
- Enable multi-factor authentication (MFA) on all accounts.
- Check financial statements for unauthorized transactions.
- Notify the relevant platform and, if necessary, report identity theft.

3. Preparing for Data Loss or Device Theft

- Regularly back up important files to external storage and cloud services.
- Use remote-wipe features on your devices to erase data in case of theft.
- Ensure your devices are encrypted to protect sensitive information.

Final Thoughts

The appendices serve as an actionable reference guide for maintaining digital wellbeing. Whether you're focusing on decluttering your digital space, improving privacy, or finding a balance between technology and real life, these resources will support your journey toward a simplified, secure, and mindful digital existence.

www.ingramcontent.com/pod-product-compliance
Lightning Source LLC
Chambersburg PA
CBHW071003050326
40689CB00014B/3465